# Yum, Yum, Y

by Katherine Gregory      illustrated by Bob Barner

### Harcourt
SCHOOL PUBLISHERS

Requests for permission to make copies of any part of the work should be addressed to School Permissions and Copyrights, Harcourt, Inc., 6277 Sea Harbor Drive, Orlando, Florida 32887-6777. Fax: 407-345-2418.

HARCOURT and the Harcourt Logo are trademarks of Harcourt, Inc., registered in the United States of America and/or other jurisdictions. Printed in the United States of America

ISBN 10  0-15-364074-X
ISBN 13  978-0-15-364074-2

3 4 5 6 7 8 9 10   179   17 16 15 14 13 12 11 10 09 08

Ordering Options
ISBN 10  0-15-364175-4
ISBN 13  978-0-15-364175-6

Gus and Bud are up.
A big nut is down there.

Gus and Bud want the nut.
Who will get it?

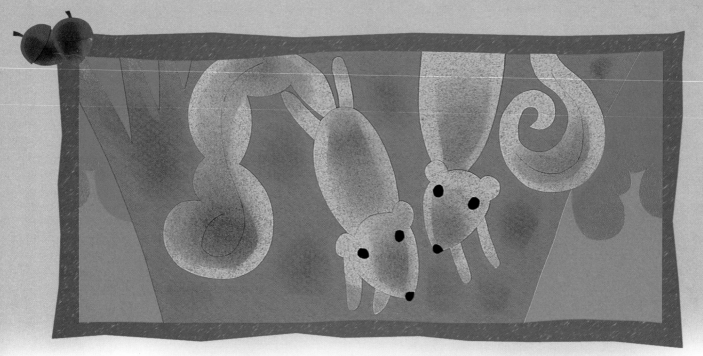

Will Gus get the nut?
Will Bud get the nut?

Gus will not get it.
Bud will not get it.

Gus and Bud fuss.

Gus and Bud tug on it.

Let Mom cut the nut.
Mom will cut it for us.

Gus and Bud will get the nut.
Yum, yum, yum!

**School-Home Connection** Have your child read the book to you.
Then discuss times when your child has shared with a friend or sibling.

. . . . . . . . . . . . . . . . . . . . . . . . . . . . . . . . . . . . . . . . . . . . . . . . . . . . . . . . . . . . .

## Yum, Yum, Yum
**Word Count:** 75

| **High-Frequency Words** | **Decodable Words\*** | |
|---|---|---|
| and | a | Mom |
| are | big | not |
| down | **Bud** | **nut** |
| for | **cut** | on |
| the | **fuss** | **tug** |
| there | get | **up** |
| want | **Gus** | **us** |
| who | is | will |
| | it | **yum** |
| | let | |

*\*Boldface words indicate sound-spelling introduced in this story.*